BUILD YOUR OWN WORKSHOP

11 Special Projects to make your workshop complete!

By the Editors of Rodale Press

Contents

Introduction

There are many times when every craftsman wishes he had an extra hand—or two. Well, here's a book full of "helping hand" projects you can build that will add extra enjoyment—not to mention ease, organization and safety—to the hours you spend in your workshop.

If you're just getting started as a woodworker or cabinetmaker, here are the plans you need to turn part of your basement or garage into a complete home workplace. We show you how to build a movable workbench with plenty of storage space, a routabout cabinet that makes routing and jointing a whole lot easier, a tool cabinet modeled on the ones found in automotive shops, sawhorses that fold and are easily hung on a wall, and more. There are projects to help your workshop "grow" with your experience and individual interests: project storage shelves, an adjustable roller stand, a welding table, a sharpening bench. In short, there's a book to keep you planning and building for years to come.

All projects feature step-by-step instructions and exploded-view diagrams to facilitate construction. And every one is a proven design, built and used by professionals. In fact, you can find benches, cabinets and workstands just like them—right here in the shops at Rodale Press.

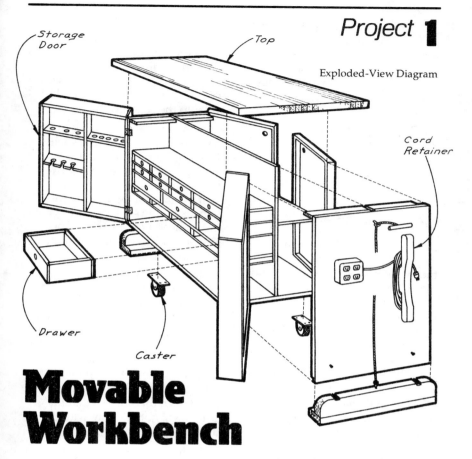

Storage Door

Top

Project **1**

Exploded-View Diagram

Cord Retainer

Drawer

Caster

Movable Workbench

An organized work space is often the key to getting projects completed. This workbench, designed for and used in the Rodale shops for several years now, practically guarantees that your shop will stay neater and more organized. The bench's large top and ample storage space provide room for most projects and tools. The casters make cleaning up chores easier and allow you to quickly rearrange your workshop to suit specific needs. Built-in kickstands lift the workbench off the casters, preventing it from rolling around when in use.

The design of the bench is so basic that it is easy to alter its dimensions to suit your requirements. You may substitute different materials if you wish (particle board or plywood, for instance, each covered with a removable sheet of tempered hardboard, makes a perfectly adequate top in lieu of the expensive hardwood butcher block top shown here). The doors may be redesigned if you desire, or left off, and the electrical outlet and vise are optional. Naturally, their location on the bench is also a matter of personal taste.

1. Follow the Cutting Diagram in order to cut all the major pieces for the bench (except the top) from a single 4 × 8-foot sheet of ¾-inch A-C or comparable grade plywood. Label each piece as it is cut.

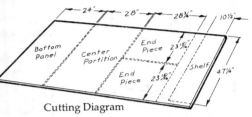

Cutting Diagram

2. Cut a rabbet ¾ inch wide by ⅜ inch deep across the bottom of the inside (rough side) of each end piece. Also cut a dado (to seat the center partition) ¾ inch wide by ⅜ inch deep down the inside of each end piece. Locate the dado, as shown in the Exploded-View Diagram, 11 inches from one side of each piece and 12¹/₁₆ inches from the other. Be sure to create a left end piece and a right end piece.

3. Sand all the pieces, including the shelf.

4. Butt the two end pieces against the center partition. Make sure all top edges are flush and that the partition seats firmly in the dadoes. Fasten the pieces together with glue and 6d finishing nails.

5. Fit the bottom panel into the rabbets on the end pieces. The upper surface of the panel should butt against the lower edge of the center divider. Glue and nail the bottom panel in place.

6. Cut four pieces of 1 × 2 (¾ × 1½-inch) stock, each 11 inches in length, for the top cleats. Install them in the cabinet by butting the

cleats even with the top edges of the end pieces and center partition, then fastening them with 6d finishing nails driven through the end pieces into the cleats. Also drive nails at an angle through the cleats and into the center partition.

7. Cut two pieces of 1 × 2 each 10 inches in length, for the shelf cleats, and install them at the convenient height in the 12¹/₁₆-inch-deep side of the cabinet. Fit the shelf in place on top of the cleats, then fasten the shelf using 1½-inch #10 flathead wood screws. The screws make it easy to adjust the shelf's height if necessary.

8. Mount 2½-inch-diameter rotating casters on the bottom panel using T-nut fasteners, bolts, and washers. Fastener sizes appropriate for most casters are ⁵/₁₆-inch T-nuts, ⁵/₁₆ × ¾-inch hex head bolts, and ⁵/₁₆-inch flat washers. Mount the casters on the bottom panel 4¼ inches from the ends and 1 inch from the sides so that the casters will not interfere with the kickstand (see step 10).

9. Cut four pieces of 2 × 4 (1½ × 3½-inch) stock, each 23 inches in length, for the two kickstands. Each kickstand is made of two pieces fastened together with glue and nails to make L-shapes as shown

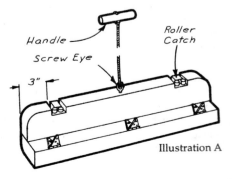

Illustration A

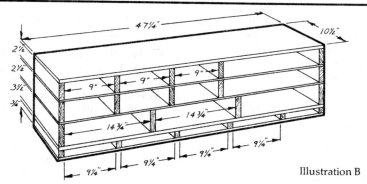

in the diagram. When joined, one side of each "L" will measure 3½ inches wide, the other 4½ inches wide. Cut dadoes in the top edge of the 4½-inch-wide side of each kickstand to accept double-roller catches. Install the catches. Also install 1½-inch screw eyes (see Illustration A).

10. Sand the kickstands and fasten them to the bottom of the work-bench with T-hinges. Be sure the ends of the stands do not protrude beyond the width of the cabinet. Mark where the roller catches touch the outside of the bench cabinet ends when the stands are in their "up" position. Install the screw-in portions of the catches at these points.

11. Handmade drawers are op-tional. Prebuilt drawers can be sub-stituted or the cabinet space filled with shelves. Should you choose to make the drawers yourself, build the drawer cabinet first, begin by cutting all the pieces to the sizes shown (see Illustration B and Cutting List). Then assemble them starting with the bottom level. Fasten the spacers to the horizontal pieces with glue and nails, then attach the next level, and so on. Be careful to keep the spacers square

to the horizontal pieces so that the drawers will fit properly.

12. When the drawer cabinet is assembled, sand it, then mount it as desired inside the workbench cabinet on the 11-inch-deep side of the center partition. Fasten the drawer cabinet securely with glue and nails. Be sure the cabinet is level.

13. Cut the pieces for the drawers, using the inside measurements of the drawer cabinet compartments as your guide. For looks and dura-bility, make the drawer fronts of pine or other solid wood. The sides, backs and bottoms can be made of solid wood or plywood. Rabbet the pieces as shown (see Illustration C), then assemble the drawers by gluing and nailing the pieces together. Drill finger holes in the drawer fronts or install standard "store-bought" pulls.

14. Check the fit of each drawer by sliding it into its compartment.

Illustration C

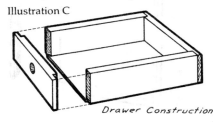

Drawer Construction

Sand off excess wood if necessary. After applying finish to the drawers and cabinet (see step 21), a coat of wax along the drawer sides will assure their smooth operation.

15. Doors can provide a lot of storage space in addition to keeping sawdust out of the drawers and shelves. The doors for this bench are two sizes: 5½ inch deep on the drawer side of the cabinet, and 1½ inch deep on the shelf side. To make them, first cut the pieces to the dimensions shown (see Illustration D). Do not cut the pieces for the center partition or shelves at this time, however. These should be cut to fit after the other parts of the doors are assembled (see step 16). Cut rabbets across the inside ends of the side pieces to accept the top and bottom pieces. Cut dadoes, ¼ inch wide by ⅜ inch deep, into all the door pieces, ¼ inch from their front edges to house the plywood door fronts.

16. Drill ½-inch-deep holes for shelf pins on the inside of each 5½-inch drawer-side piece. Locate the holes on each pair of sides identically so that the shelves will be level when fitted. Space the holes at intervals as desired so the shelves may be adjusted up or down.

17. Test fit all the pieces of the doors, then glue and nail them together. Nails are not necessary for fastening the plywood door fronts; glue alone will hold them securely in place.

18. Now cut the center partition for one 5½-inch-wide door carefully, so that it fits vertically between the door top and bottom, and can be fastened without pulling those pieces out of square. Drill shelf pin holes entirely through the 5-inch-wide partition piece, using the same measurements and spacing as for the holes drilled earlier in the 5½-inch-wide door sides. Fasten the center partition in place with glue and nails.

19. Cut shelves to size from pine or plywood to fit between the partition in the 5½-inch-wide door and to fit the unpartitioned 5½-inch-wide door. Drill holes in each shelf to hold tools which can be hung by their handles (such as screwdrivers and chisels), then mount the shelves in place using shelf pins. After testing the fit, remove the shelves and pins until after the doors have been finished (see step 21).

Illustration D

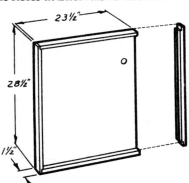

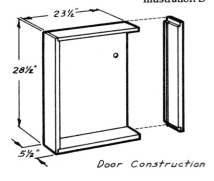

Door Construction

20. As an option for the 1½-inch-wide doors, cut shelves of narrow stock and fit them as in the previous step. Fasten the shelves in place with nails. These shelves also may be drilled and used to hold small items such as awls or spade bits.

21. Apply finish to the workbench cabinet kickstands, drawer cabinet, drawers, shelves and doors. Mount a homemade rope pull to each kickstand by securing the rope ends through the screw eyes (see Illustration A).

22. Mount the bench top. First, position it to overhang the bench cabinet as shown in the diagram —or to suit—then clamp or have someone hold it securely in place while you drill pilot holes from underneath, through the cleats at each end of the bench cabinet and into the underside of the top. Then fasten the top to the bench cabinet using eight 1½-inch #14 flathead wood screws.

23. Attach the doors to the bench cabinet sides using two ¾-inch offset hinges per door. Be sure to attach the doors so their bottom edges are even with the bottom edge of the workbench. As an option, one or more of the doors can be made detachable for use as a portable tool rack by using loose joint hinges instead of the standard fixed-pin variety. Mount the doors about 2 inches lower than the bench top so that when you need to, you can simply lift the door off the hinges. Use the movable drawer, or drawers, to stack groups of specialty tools used for single operations, such as tools for electrical or plumbing jobs. Also install catches—magnetic, double-roller, or hook-and-eye —to the doors and bench cabinet to keep the doors closed. If you wish, attach hasps to the door for use with a padlock.

24. You may also wish to mount an electrical outlet to the workbench. This is very convenient, making it easy to use power tools without searching for extension cords. It also allows you to keep a lamp or even a radio on the bench without difficulty. Attach a four-gang receptacle to the side of the bench, then plug everything in there. Instead of four extension cords going from individual tools to the wall, only one—from the receptacle—is needed.

Shopping List

Lumber

1	pc. 2" x 4" x 8'	5	pcs. 1" x 3" x 8'
1	pc. 1" x 12" x 8'	3	pcs. 1" x 2" x 8'
1	pc. 1" x 6" x" 10'	1	pc. 1" x 1" x 8' (baluster stock)
2	pcs. 1" x 6" x 8'		
1	pc. 1" x 4" x 10'	1	pc. 1½" x 32" x 62" (laminated stock)
1	pc. 1" x 4" x 8'		

Plywood

1	sheet ¾″ x 4′ x 8′ A-C Grade		2	sheets ¼″ x 4′ x 8′ A-C Grade

Hardware

4	Casters 2½″		4	Flathead Wood Screws 1½″ x #10
16	Hex-Head Bolts ⁵⁄₁₆–18 x ¾″		1	lb. Finishing Nails 6d
16	T-nuts ⁵⁄₁₆″–18		1	Double Receptacle Box
2	Screw Eyes ³⁄₁₆″ x 1½″		2	Receptacles
4	T-hinges 2″		1	Wire 16–3 x 25′
8	Cabinet Hinges ¾″ x 2″		1	Plug
8	Flathead Wood Screws 1½″ x #14		4	Magnetic Catches 1″
			4	Roller Catches 1¼″
10	Flathead Wood Screws 3½″ x #10		16	Flat Washers ⁵⁄₁₆″

Lumber Cutting List

Size	Piece	Quantity
2 x 4		
1½″ x 3½″ x 23″	Kickstands	4
1 x 12		
¾″ x 10½″ x 47¼″	Drawer Cabinet Top and Bottom	2
1 x 6		
¾″ x 5½″ x 28½″	Door Sides	4
¾″ x 5½″ x 23½″	Door Tops and Bottoms	4
¾″ x 5″ x 27″	Door Partition	1
¾″ x 5″ x 22⅝″	Door Shelves	2
¾″ x 5″ x 10⅞″	Door Shelves	2
1 x 4		
¾″ x 3⅜″ x 9¾″	Drawer Sides	6
¾″ x 3⅜″ x 14⅝″	Drawer Fronts and Backs	6
¾″ x 3½″ x 10½″	Drawer Spacers	4

Size	Piece	Quantity
1 x 3		
¾" x 2½" x 10½"	Drawer Spacers	10
¾" x 2⅜" x 9¾"	Drawer Sides	16
¾" x 2⅜" x 8⅞"	Drawer Fronts and Backs	12
¾" x 2⅜" x 16⅜"	Drawer Fronts and Backs	4
1 x 2		
¾" x 1½" x 11"	Top Cleats	4
¾" x 1½" x 10"	Shelf Cleats	2
¾" x 1½" x 28½"	Door Sides	4
¾" x 1½" x 23½"	Door Tops and Bottoms	4
1 x 1 (Baluster Stock)		
¾" x ¾" x 10½"	Drawer Cabinet Spacers	6
Laminated Stock		
1½" x 32" x 62"	Bench Top	1
¾-inch A-C Plywood		
¾" x 24" x 48"	Cabinet Bottom	1
¾" x 28" x 48"	Center Partition	1
¾" x 23 ¹⁵⁄₁₆" x 28¾"	Cabinet Ends	2
¾" x 10½" x 47¼"	Shelf	1
¼-inch A-C Plywood		
¼" x 23½" x 27¾"	Door Panels	4
¼" x 10½" x 47¼"	Drawer Supports	3
¼" x 8⅛" x 9¾"	Drawer Bottoms	6
¼" x 9¾" x 15⅝"	Drawer Bottoms	2
¼" x 9¾" x 13⅞"	Drawer Bottoms	3

Project 2

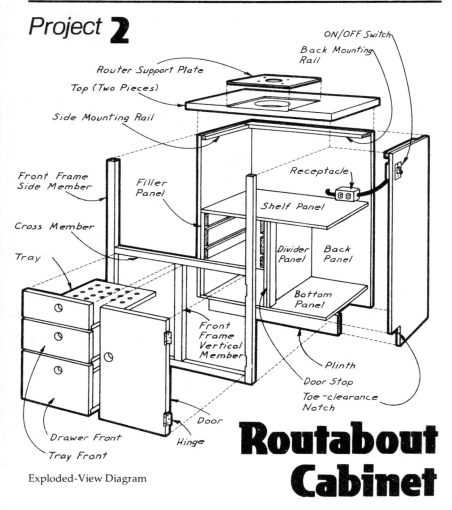

ON/OFF Switch
Back Mounting Rail
Router Support Plate
Top (Two Pieces)
Side Mounting Rail
Receptacle
Front Frame Side Member
Filler Panel
Shelf Panel
Cross Member
Divider Panel
Back Panel
Tray
Bottom Panel
Front Frame Vertical Member
Plinth
Door Stop
Toe-clearance Notch
Drawer Front
Tray Front
Hinge
Door

Exploded-View Diagram

Routabout Cabinet

The routabout cabinet, designed by the Rodale Press Design Group, has been in daily use in our shop for over three years. It's handy and versatile. The router is solidly mounted upside-down underneath the cabinet top. You move the wood past the spinning bit which protrudes above the surface, instead of attempting to steer the unwieldy router itself along the edge of your clamped-down board. Set-up time for straight cuts, such as dadoes and rabbets, is reduced also, compared with a hand-held router, since guides can easily be clamped to the cabinet top. The routabout cabinet also offers lots of additional storage room for router bits, wrenches and guides, plus space for circular saws, drills and other shop tools.

Although a cabinet-mounted router is safer than a hand-held

router, you must still be extremely careful when using it. The danger caused by a bit spinning at several thousand rpm is ever present when the router is plugged in. Always be wary of what a router can do to careless fingers. Follow all the safety precautions recommended by the manufacturer. Wear eye protection, use the right bits, be careful of loose-fitting clothing and have adequate lighting. In addition, always use a push stick (as you would with a table saw) to feed narrow lumber past the bit and do not rout pieces that are less than 2 inches long.

1. Cut two pieces of ½-inch plywood to 17 × 33¼ inches each for the side panels. Cut a 3-inch-deep by 3½-inch-high toe-clearance notch from a corner of each side panel, as shown in the Exploded-View Diagram.

2. Cut two pieces of ½-inch plywood to 17 × 22⅝ inches each for the bottom and shelf, and two pieces to 17 × 15⅞ inches each for the divider and filler panels. The filler panel is necessary only if the tray and drawer are installed (see step 27).

3. Cut two pieces of ½-inch plywood to 19½ × 29 inches each for the double-layer top. Glue the pieces for the top together with carpenter's wood glue.

4. Cut one piece of ¼-inch plywood to 24 × 33 inches for the back panel. Note that the back panel is ¼-inch plywood, not ½-inch plywood.

5. Cut one piece of 1 × 4 (¾ × 3½-inch) stock to 23 inches for the

back mounting rail, one piece of 1 × 4 to 24 inches for the plinth and two pieces of 1 × 1 (¾ × ¾-inch) stock to 13½ inches each for the side mounting rails.

6. Now cut two pieces of 1 × 2 (¾ × 1½-inch) stock to 1¼ × 30¾ inches each for the front frame side members, two pieces of 1 × 2 to 1¼ × 21⅛ inches each for the front frame cross members and one piece of 1 × 2 to 1¼ × 15¼ inches for the front frame vertical member.

7. Cut a piece of aluminum sheet to ⅛ × 12 × 12 inches for the router-support plate.

8. Assemble the main cabinet pieces, as shown in Illustration A, with carpenter's wood glue and 6d finishing nails. First assemble the shelf to the top edge of the divider panel. Then assemble the bottom panel to the divider panel and finally, fasten the side panels to the shelf and bottom panels.

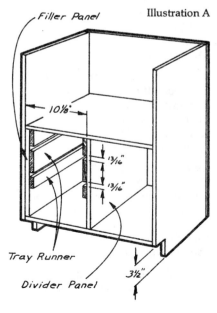

Filler Panel

Illustration A

10⅛"

1³⁄₁₆"

1³⁄₁₆"

Tray Runner

Divider Panel

3½"

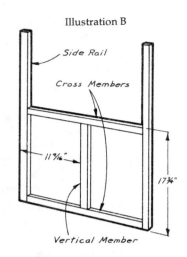

Illustration B

Side Rail

Cross Members

11 9/16"

17¾"

Vertical Member

accept 1½-inch #8 mounting screws. Drill from the bottom, in the positions shown in Illustration C.

15. Center the double-layer top panel on the router cabinet and drill 1½-inch #8 pilot holes into the top to accept the mounting screws. Secure the top to the cabinet with 1½-inch #8 flathead wood screws.

16. Cut edging and a top panel of plastic laminate from a 24 × 36-inch sheet of laminate. Apply the laminate to the cabinet top with contact cement.

17. Rout a ⅛ × 12 × 12-inch area into the cabinet top as shown in Illustration C to accept the router mounting plate.

18. Measure the diameter of your router's base, then cut a hole whose diameter is ½ inch larger than this in the center of the routed area. The extra space provides clearance to mount and demount the router.

19. Install the router mounting plate in the routed area, then drill and countersink holes in the corners of the plate to accept #8 flathead wood screws. Drill ³/₃₂-inch-diameter pilot holes through the countersunk holes and into the cabinet top. Secure the router plate

9. Square the cabinet, then fasten the back panel in place with carpenter's wood glue and 4d finishing nails.

10. Fasten the back and side mounting rails to the back and side panels with carpenter's wood glue and 4d finishing nails.

11. Fasten the plinth to the front of the cabinet, as shown, with carpenter's wood glue and 6d finishing nails.

12. Assemble the front frame side members, the cross members and the vertical members, as shown in Illustration B, with carpenter's wood glue and 6d finishing nails. Allow the glue to set.

13. Align the top of the side mounting rails so they are flush with the tops of the side panels, and the horizontal members flush with the shelf and bottom panel, then fasten the front frame to the cabinet with 6d finishing nails.

14. Drill and countersink holes through the mounting rails to

Illustration C

Top

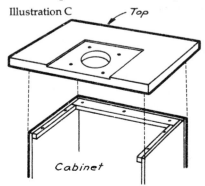

Cabinet

to the cabinet with 1-inch #8 flat-head wood screws.

20. Cut a 1½-inch-diameter hole in the center of the router mounting plate. This size hole is large enough to safely hold all but the largest router bits yet still provide adequate clearance.

21. Center the router base over the hole in the router mounting plate, while holding the router right-side-up on top of the plate. Mark where the router mounting holes must be drilled. The number, size and placement of the holes is specific to your router. Drill the holes, then countersink them to accept the heads of the mounting screws.

22. Mount the router upside-down against the bottom surface of the router mounting plate using machine screws to fit your router. The heads of the screws must be either flush with or recessed below the surface of the mounting plate.

23. Determine the best place for the cabinet switch, or place it as shown in the Exploded-View Diagram, and cut the switch box hole. Install the box, wiring and switch.

24. Install a second box for a duplex receptacle. Install the box, then wire the receptacle to the switch according to the wiring diagram. Install a 3-prong plug to the wire.

25. The router is now ready for use, and can be used to build the trays, drawers and door, plus any other storage spaces.

26. Cut two pieces of 1 × 4 stock to 2¾ × 17 inches each, two pieces of 1 × 4 to 3⅛ × 17 inches each and two pieces of 1 × 4 to 1⅝ × 17 inches each for the tray runners.

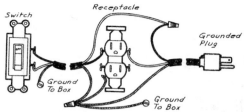

Illustration D

27. Install the runners in the positions shown in Illustration A, with carpenter's wood glue and 3d finishing nails. Maintain a 1⅛-inch space between the runners to provide adequate clearance for the tray bottoms.

28. Cut one piece of 1 × 4 stock to 2⅞ × 10⅛ inches and one piece of 1 × 6 (¾ × 5½-inch) stock to 4¼ × 10⅛ inches for the top and middle tray fronts.

29. Cut one piece of 1 × 10 (¾ × 9¼-inch) stock to 7¾ × 10⅛ inches for the drawer front, one piece of 1 × 6 to 3¼ × 8⅝ inches for the drawer back and two pieces of 1 × 6 to 4¼ × 17¼ inches each for the drawer sides.

30. Cut four pieces of ½-inch plywood to 10 × 17¼ inches each for the tray bottoms, and one piece to 9⅜ × 17¼ inches for the drawer bottom.

31. Set up a guide, and cut a ⅜-inch-deep by 1-inch-wide rabbet into the bottom inside edges of the drawer and tray fronts to fit the bottom pieces. (Then, drill 1-inch-diameter finger holes through the drawer and tray fronts in the positions shown in Illustration E.)

32. On the drawer front only, rout a ⅜-inch-deep by ½-inch-wide rabbet on each side edge of the

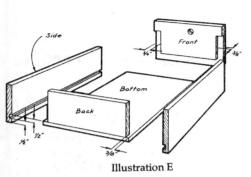

Illustration E

drawer front, as shown in Illustration E.

33. On the drawer sides only, rout a 3/8-inch-deep by 1/2-inch-wide dado, along the drawer sides 1/2 inch from the bottom edges. The dado, when the drawer is assembled, will be on the inside of the drawer as shown in Illustration E.

34. Assemble the drawer front to the bottom, sides and back with carpenter's wood glue and 6d finishing nails.

35. Drill holes in two of the tray bottom pieces to store bits and other accessories. Then, glue the drilled bottom pieces to the undrilled bottom pieces with carpenter's wood glue and 6d finishing nails. Sand the trays and drawer, then apply an appropriate finish.

36. Cut one piece of 1/2-inch plywood to 10 1/8 × 15 1/8 inches for the door, and one piece of 1 × 2 stock to 15 7/8 inches for the door stop.

37. Cut mortises in the door to fit 1/2 × 2-inch cabinet hinges in the positions shown in the Exploded-View Diagram. Install the hinges in the mortises and install the door to the cabinet. Drill a 1-inch-diameter finger hole in a convenient position. Install a magnetic catch, or one of another suitable design, to the door and cabinet.

38. Install the drawer and trays, then apply finish to the remaining cabinet parts.

Shopping List

Lumber

1	pc. 1" x 10" x 1'		1	pc. 1" x 2" x 8'
1	pc. 1" x 6" x 6'		1	pc. 1" x 2" x 6'
1	pc. 1" x 4" x 8'		1	pc. 1" x 1" x 3' (baluster stock)
1	pc. 1" x 4" x 6'			

Plywood

1	sheet 1/2" x 4' x 8'		1	pc. 1/4" x 2' x 4'

Aluminum Sheet

1	Router Mounting Plate 1/8" x 12" x 12"

Plastic Laminate

1 Top Surface ³⁄₁₆″ x 24″ x 36″

Hardware

25′	Wire with Ground 14–2 Gauge	1	Grounded Plug
1	Receptacle Box 2″ x 4″	1	Duplex Cover Plate
1	Switch Box 2″ x 4″	1	lb. Finishing Nails 6d
1	Single Pole Switch	½	lb. Finishing Nails 4d
1	Grounded Receptacle	4	Flathead Wood Screws 1½″ x #8

Lumber Cutting List

Size	Piece	Quantity
1 x 10		
¾″ x 7¾″ x 10⅛″	Drawer Front	1
1 x 6		
¾″ x 4¼″ x 17¼″	Drawer Sides	2
¾″ x 3¼″ x 8⅝″	Drawer Back	1
¾″ x 4¼″ x 10⅛″	Middle Tray Front	1
1 x 4		
¾″ x 3½″ x 24″	Plinth	1
¾″ x 3½″ x 23″	Back Mounting Rail	1
¾″ x 3⅛″ x 17″	Middle Runners	2
¾″ x 2⅞″ x 10⅛″	Top Tray Front	1
¾″ x 2¾″ x 17″	Top Runners	2
¾″ x 1⅝″ x 17″	Bottom Runners	2
1 x 2		
¾″ x 1¼″ x 30¾″	Side Members	2
¾″ x 1¼″ x 21⅛″	Cross Members	2
¾″ x 1¼″ x 15¼″	Vertical Member	1
¾″ x 1½″ x 15⅞″	Door Stop	1
1 x 1 (Baluster Stock)		
¾″ x ¾″ x 13½″	Side Mounting Rail	2

Size	Piece	Quantity
Plywood		
½" x 17" x 33¼"	Side Panels	2
½" x 17" x 22⅝"	Bottom Panel	1
½" x 17" x 22⅝"	Shelf Panel	1
½" x 17" x 15⅞"	Divider Panel	1
½" x 17" x 15⅞"	Filler Panel	1
½" x 19½" x 29"	Top Panels	2
½" x 9⅜" x 17¼"	Drawer Bottom (Dadoed Front Piece)	1
⅝" x 10" x 17¼"	Tray Bottoms	2
⅝" x 10⅛" x 15⅛"	Door	1
¼" x 24" x 33"	Back Panel	1

Note: Lumber must be ripped to specific widths.

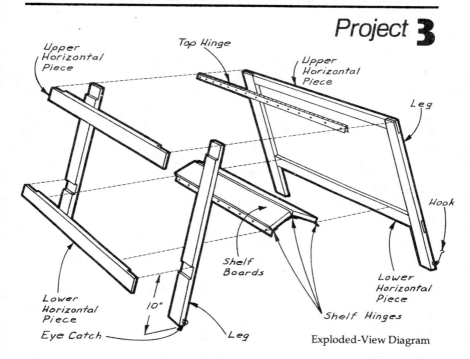

Exploded-View Diagram

Lightweight Sawhorses

These lightweight, folding sawhorses hang on a wall when not in use, or store away neatly in a small amount of space. They are at least half the weight of conventional sawhorses—almost anyone can handle a pair of them easily—yet they hold as much weight as the conventional type.

The materials used to construct them are ¾-inch-thick stock and continuous hinges also known as piano hinges. New piano hinges can be expensive. If you can't salvage any, use butt or strap hinges instead. Purchase plain steel hinges,

not brass or brass plated. (The hinges are concealed when the sawhorses are assembled, and steel is less expensive and also stronger than brass.) Add hook-and-eye fasteners to the sawhorses to keep the legs closed when in storage.

In use, the hinged split shelf underneath the sawhorse locks into place and makes the horses rigid. This shelf can also support a toolbox. The two side frames of the sawhorse are held together at the top by the continuous hinge. You must be careful not to cut into the top hinge when using the sawhorses, since the hinge is very near the surface. To be safe, use 2 × 4's laid on to of the sawhorses as spacers when cutting large pancels or ripping lumber.

Sawhorses should fit the height of the user. Illustration A shows dimensions for a popular sawhorse size of 28 inches. Note that the actual length of the legs is always slightly greater than the height of the finished horse. This is because each leg represents the hypotenuse of a right triangle formed as also shown.

The length of the sawhorses shown here is 42 inches. This can easily be altered without changing the geometry of the legs presented in the plans. In fact, these sawhorses are so easy to build, especially after you've made the first set, you might want to build several pairs in different heights and sizes to accommodate different operations.

The instructions that follow are for building sawhorses that are 28 inches high. The text and materials chart list the number of pieces to build one sawhorse. To build a pair, merely double the number of pieces.

1. Cut four pieces of 1 × 4(¾ × 3½-inch) stock to 28¾ inches each for the legs. Make certain they are all of equal length and that the ends are square before proceeding.

2. Cut four pieces of 1 × 4 stock to 42 inches each for the upper and lower horizontal pieces.

3. Rip a 6-foot length of 1 × 6 (¾ × 5½-inch) stock to 4½ inches in width, then cut the board into two pieces, each 31 inches in length for the shelves.

Illustration A

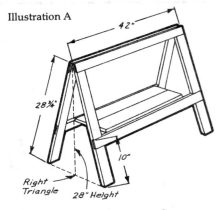

4. Cut one piece of 1 × 1-inch continuous hinge to 36 inches in length for the top hinge, and three pieces of 1 × 1-inch hinge each to 12 inches in length for the shelf hinges.

5. Cut half-lap joints in the legs and horizontal pieces where indicated in the Exploded-View Diagram. Use the actual pieces being joined to mark the half-laps, and make the joints as tight as possible since they determine much of the sawhorse's strength. A diagram of a half-lap joint is shown in Illustration B. Half-laps are made by laying the pieces to be joined across each other at right angles (or at whatever angle the plans call for them to overlap) and just scribing the width of each piece onto the other, then carefully chiseling away precisely half the thickness of each piece, within the area of the scribed lines. The pieces are then joined with glue, and screws for extra strength.

6. Cut a 20-degree bevel on the leg bottoms so they rest flat on the floor. Be certain that the bevel is cut on the inside face of the legs.

7. Position the legs and horizontal pieces together to form two frames,

one for each side of the sawhorses. Apply carpenter's wood glue to the joints, clamp them, and install two ⅝-inch #8 flathead wood screws in each. (Use a ³/₃₂-inch bit to drill the pilot holes.) When assembled, both frames should match closely.

8. When dry, lay the two side frames on a flat surface with the inside faces up and the top edges butted together. Position the 36-inch continuous hinge over the seam formed by the butted upper horizontal pieces of the frames and mark locations for mounting new pilot holes. Be sure to fit the hinge so that when assembled, the frames will fold flat against each other. Drill the pilot holes (their size depends on the screws supplied with the hinge) and secure the hinge to each side frame, as shown in the Exploded-View Diagram. When finished, fold the frames together to check your work. Slight bending of the hinge along its length is possible if minor adjustment is necessary.

9. Position the two shelf boards edge to edge. Be sure their ends are flush. As you did in the previous step, lay a 12-inch length of continuous hinge over the seam formed by the two boards and mark locations for mounting screw holes. To properly fit this hinge, it should fasten to the underside of the finished shelf and close completely when the boards are face to face and the sawhorse is folded up. The hinge should open out when the boards are edge to edge and the sawhorse is in use. Drill the pilot holes, then mount the hinge.

10. Lay the hinged shelf boards flat, with their hinged side facing up. Flush with the outside edge of each board attach a 12-inch length of continuous hinge, oriented so that when the sawhorse is open the leaves of the hinge will form an angle, as shown in the Exploded-View Diagram, and when the sawhorse is closed the hinge will lie flat.

11. Prop the sawhorse side frames open and hold the shelf assembly in position against the upper inside edges of the lower horizontal frame pieces. On the inside faces of the frame pieces, mark the locations of the unattached hinge leaves and mounting screw holes. (The unattached leaves should point toward the floor.) Remove the shelf assembly, drill pilot holes in the frame pieces, and reattach the shelf permanently, using the screws provided for mounting the hinges.

12. Close the sawhorse and install a 1-inch-long hook-and-eye fastener across one pair of legs to keep the sawhorse closed during storage and transport.

Illustration B

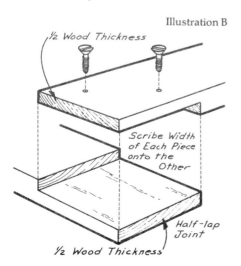

½ Wood Thickness

Scribe Width
of Each Piece
onto the
Other

Half-lap
Joint

½ Wood Thickness

Shopping List

Lumber

4 pcs. 1″ x 4″ x 8′

1 pc. 1″ x 6″ x 6′

Hardware

1 Top Hinge with screws 1″ x 1″ x 36″

3 Shelf Hinges with screws 1″ x 1″ x 12″

32 Flathead Wood Screws ⅝″ x #8

1 Hook-and-Eye Fastener 1″

Lumber Cutting List

Size	*Piece*	*Quantity*
1 x 4		
¾″ x 3½″ x 30¾″	Legs	4
¾″ x 3½″ x 42″	Horizontal Pieces	4
1 x 6		
¾″ x 4½″ x 31″	Shelf	2

Project 4

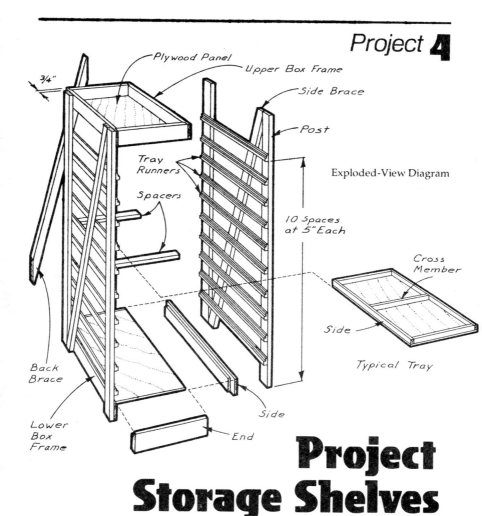

Plywood Panel

Upper Box Frame

Side Brace

3/4"

Post

Tray Runners

Exploded-View Diagram

Spacers

10 Spaces at 5" Each

Cross Member

Side

Typical Tray

Back Brace

Side

End

Lower Box Frame

Project Storage Shelves

Here's a handy shelf arrangement based on the kind bakers use to store fresh goods or unbaked items waiting for the oven. Its purpose is to provide a place to stash unfinished projects so your workbench can be kept free for more pressing needs (or just as likely, more projects to be left unfinished!). The Rodale Design Group built the unit based on plans by one of our editors, and put it to immediate use

in their shop. There it's referred to as "the back burner."

The rack has runners to hold nine trays. The instructions, however, call for building only seven, since some items to be stored will undoubtedly be tall and require extra height. The framework of the rack and trays is #2 pine. The panels for the box frames and tray bottoms are all cut from a single sheet of 1/4-inch plywood. Since our shelves are for shop use we left them unfinished. If you choose to paint yours, be careful not to get paint on the rabbeted parts of the runners or on the lower edges of the trays, either of which might interfere with their smooth sliding action.

1. Cut 20 pieces of 1 × 2 (¾ × 1½-inch) stock, each 32 inches in length for tray runners. Then cut a ½ × ½-inch rabbet along the length of each runner.

2. Cut four pieces of 1 × 2 stock to 60 inches each for posts. Starting from the lower end make a mark on one face every 5 inches along the length of each post until ten marks have been made. Spread the posts apart in parallel pairs. Place the runners across them, with the rabbeted edges up, as shown in the Exploded-View Diagram, and the bottom edges on the marks. Align the ends of the runners flush with the outside edges of the posts. Fasten the runners to the posts using carpenter's wood glue and 1¼-inch drywall nails.

3. Cut two pieces of 1 × 2 stock to 67 inches each for side braces. Lay each brace diagonally across the

outsides of the runners between the attached posts as shown in the Exploded-View Diagram, and fasten them with carpenter's wood glue and 1¼-inch drywall nails. For appearance's sake, drive the drywall nails from inside the frame, through the runners into the braces, so they will not be visible from the outside. You may mark and pre-cut the ends of the braces first or glue and nail them in place and trim the ends afterwards.

4. Cut four pieces of 1 × 4 (¾ × 3½-inch) stock to 32¾ inches each for box frame sides. Then cut a ⅜-inch deep rabbet ¾ inch wide across the ends on one face of each piece, and a ¼-inch-wide rabbet ⅜ inch deep along one edge on the same side of the piece as the rabbets, as shown in the Exploded-View Diagram.

5. Cut four pieces of 1 × 4 stock to 16 inches each for box frame ends. Then cut a ¼-inch-wide rabbet ⅜ inch deep along one edge of each piece.

6. Fasten the frame sides and ends together with wood glue and 6d cement-coated box nails to form

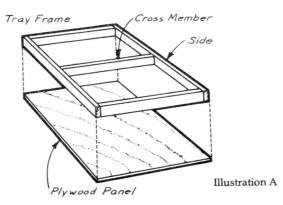

Tray Frame   Cross Member   Side

Plywood Panel   Illustration A

the upper and lower box frames, as shown in the Exploded-View Diagram. Make sure that the rabbeted edges of each set of frame pieces contact each other and face the inside of the box.

7. Divide one 4 × 8-foot sheet of ¼-inch plywood into nine equal pieces, each as close as possible to 16 × 32 inches. Fasten one panel into the rabbeted edge of each box frame using wood glue and 1¼-inch drywall nails.

8. Fasten the post and runner assemblies to the sides of the box frames. Position the box frames so that the panels of each face toward each other, and so their fronts are flush with the front edges of the post assemblies. The outer edges of each box frame should also be made flush with the ends of the posts. Fasten the posts to the boxes with wood glue and 6d cement-coated box nails.

9. Cut one piece of 1 × 2 stock to 58 inches in length for the back brace. Position it diagonally across the back of the rear posts, making use of as much of its length as possible, then fasten it to the posts using wood glue and 6d cement-coated box nails. Trim the ends of the brace flush with the posts. (If you prefer, you can mark and pre-cut the brace, before fastening it in place.)

10. Cut 14 pieces of 1 × 2 stock to 32 inches each for tray sides. Then cut 21 pieces to 14½ inches each for cross members. Fasten one cross member between each end of a pair of sides and another cross member at the center as shown in Illustration A. Use wood glue and 6d cement-coated box nails. Fasten a plywood panel to the bottom of each tray with wood glue and 1¼-inch underlayment nails.

11. Cut two pieces of 1 × 2 stock to 15¼ inches each for spacers. Glue and nail the spacers between the sixth pair of runners (counting from the bottom) to give the shelf structure more rigidity. Fasten the spacers out of the way of a tray sliding on those runners. Use wood glue and 6d cement-coated box nails.

Shopping List

Lumber

| 2 | pcs. 1" x 4" x 10' | 21 | pcs. 1" x 2" x 8' |

Plywood

| 1 | sheet ¼" x 4' x 8' |

Hardware

| ¾ | lb. Cement-Coated Box Nails 6d | 1 | pt. Carpenter's Wood Glue |
| 1 | lb. Underlayment Nails 1¼" | | |

Lumber Cutting List

Size	Piece	Quantity
1 x 4		
¾" x 3½" x 32¾"	Box Frame Sides	4
¾" x 3½" x 16"	Box Frame Ends	4
1 x 2		
¾" x 1½" x 67"	Side Braces	2
¾" x 1½" x 60"	Posts	4
¾" x 1½" x 58"	Back Brace	1
¾" x 1½" x 32"	Tray Runners	20
¾" x 1½" x 32"	Tray Sides	14
¾" x 1½" x 15¼"	Spacers	2
¾" x 1½" x 14½"	Tray Cross Members	21
¼-inch Plywood		
¼" x 16" x 32"	Box Frame and Tray Panels	9

Project 5

Adjustable Roller Stand

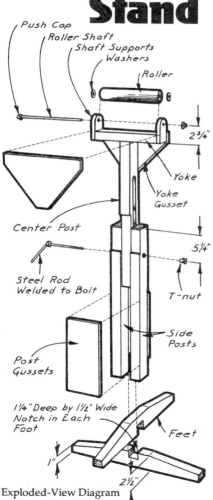

Push Cap
Roller Shaft
Shaft Supports
Washers
Roller
2¾"
Yoke
Yoke Gusset
Center Post
5¼"
Steel Rod Welded to Bolt
T-nut
Side Posts
Post Gussets
1¼" Deep by 1½" Wide Notch in Each Foot
Feet
1"
2½"

Exploded-View Diagram

This lightweight, portable roller stand—designed by the Rodale Design Group for use in its own shop —-is a great help when feeding large sheets of plywood or long lengths of lumber through stationary woodworking machines where alignment and control of workpieces is critical. Use it to accompany table saw, band saw, jointer, shaper, or even drill press operations. The extra support provided by the stand helps increase the accuracy of your work and vastly improves safety.

The roller in this stand is taken from a regular cook's rolling pin. We simply removed the wooden handles, shortened the steel shaft, and mounted the roller between supports at the top of the stand. The roller we used measures $9^{13}/_{16}$ inches in length and 2 inches in diameter. Before you begin work on your roller stand, you should obtain the roller you intend to use. If its size is different from the one shown here, alter the sizes of the stand's shaft supports and yoke accordingly. Our roller also has a steel shaft and bearings. We recommend that you purchase one of similar construction to ensure that the roller stand you will build will give you years of satisfaction.

The roller itself adjusts in height, thanks to a slotted center post and handy clamping device. If you mark and label the post with the heights and names of your own stationary power tools, then when you are busily involved with a project you'll have no trouble moving the stand from machine to machine and readjusting it quickly without having to measure. For wide stock, use the roller stand as an auxiliary table beside the tool. For long lengths, position the stand at either the in-feed or outfeed side. For some jobs, especially if you work alone, you may find it convenient to use two stands, or even three.

1. Cut a piece of 2 × 2 (1½ × 1½-inch) stock to 10 inches in length for the roller stand yoke.

2. Cut two pieces of ⅝-inch plywood to 1½ × 3½ inches each for the roller shaft supports. Choose one end of each to be the top and cut a ¾-inch radius on that end.

3. Centered on a point 2¾ inches from the bottom (square) end, drill a ¼-inch-diameter hole through each shaft support to receive the ends of the roller shaft. Take care to make the holes perpendicular to the face of each piece.

4. Position the shaft supports at each end of the yoke by making sure the bottoms and sides of the supports are flush with the bottom and sides of the yoke. Then glue and nail the shaft supports to the ends of the yoke with carpenter's wood glue and 8d finish nails, as shown in the Exploded-View Diagram.

5. Cut a straight and relatively knot-free piece of 2 × 2 stock to 25½ inches in length to use as the sliding center post. Cut two pieces of straight 2 × 2 stock to 28 inches each for the side posts. Pick a top, bottom, front, and back for each post. Label them for future reference.

6. Measure 5⅛ inches from the top of the center post down one side and mark that point. Make another mark 17½ inches down from the top of the post. With a square, draw straight lines across the side of the post at those two points. Find the center of each line and drill a ⅜-inch-diameter hole through the post at both points.

7. Connect the two holes drilled in the previous step with straight lines to form the outline for a ⅜-inch-wide slot running down the sides of the center post. Cut out the slot with a saber saw or router. Make sure the slot is sufficiently straight and smooth to allow for raising and lowering the post when the stand is assembled.

8. Measure 5¼ inches from the top down one side of each side post. Square a line across each post at that point. At the centerpoint of each line, drill a ⅜-inch-diameter hole straight through each post to house the bolt and T-nut assembly to be added in step 22.

9. For smooth operation when assembled, the thickness of the top 5 inches of the two side posts and the bottom 12¾ inches of the center post need to be reduced by 1/16 inch each. This should be done on either the front or back or a combination of front and back of each post, as shown in Illustration A. Use a hand plane, sander, or another tool of your choice.

10. Center the yoke at the top end of the center post, making sure that the roller shaft supports point upward and that the yoke is correctly positioned in relation to the center post slots, as shown in the Exploded-View Diagram. Glue and nail the yoke onto the end of the center post in this position. Use 8d finishing nails.

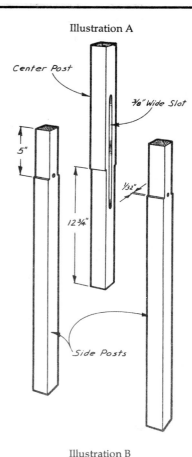

Illustration A

Center Post

³⁄₈" Wide Slot

5"

¹⁄₃₂"

12 ³⁄₄"

Side Posts

Illustration B

11 ¹⁄₄"

1 ¹⁄₂"

6 ³⁄₈"

1 ¹⁄₂"

Yoke Gusset

11. Cut two pieces of ¹⁄₄-inch plywood to 6³⁄₈ × 11¹⁄₄ inches each for the yoke gussets. Trim both to the shape shown in Illustration B.

Glue and nail the yoke gussets to the front and back of the yoke and post assembly as shown in the Exploded-View Diagram, using 1-inch underlayment nails.

12. Now remove the handles and the steel shaft from the rolling pin. Cut the steel shaft to 11³⁄₄ inches in length.

13. Attach the roller as shown in the Exploded-View Diagram. First, thread the steel shaft through one support, then through a single ¹⁄₄-inch-diameter flat washer. Next, slide the roller onto the shaft, followed by a second ¹⁄₄-inch-diameter flat washer. Finally, thread the shaft through the remaining support and fit a ¹⁄₄-inch push cap on each end of the shaft to hold the roller in place.

14. Cut two pieces of 2 × 3 (1¹⁄₂ × 2¹⁄₂-inch) stock to 24 inches each for the feet of the stand. Taper the ends as shown in the Exploded-View Diagram.

15. With the tapered edges of the feet facing up, cross the pieces at right angles on their centers. Mark and cut a half-lap joint, then fit the feet together so they form a base that will sit squarely on a flat surface. Glue the feet together using carpenter's wood glue.

16. Cut two pieces of ¹⁄₄-inch plywood to 4³⁄₈ × 12 inches each for the post gussets.

17. Assemble the side posts and center post together side-by-side, with the center post in the middle and the front faces of all three posts facing up. Position one post gusset across the posts so that the lower edge of the gusset is 3¹⁄₄ inches

from the bottom of the posts and the sides of both the gusset and the posts are flush.

18. Apply a small amount of glue to the side posts only, beneath the gussets—the center post must remain entirely free of glue in order to slide freely when the assembly is completed—then fasten the gusset in place by driving 1-inch underlayment nails through the gusset into the side post. Be careful to avoid nailing into the center post. When finished, turn the assembly over and install the remaining gusset using the same procedures.

19. Now slip the finished post assembly into place over one of the crossed feet of the base, as close to the joint itself as possible. Check that each side post contacts a pair of feet at right angles, then fasten the post assembly to the base using 8d finishing nails.

20. Sand the roller stand, being careful to round over any sharp edges. Apply a light coat of finish if desired. Finish is not necessary, but if you do use it, be sure that the parts of the stand remain free to slide afterward.

21. Add cork or nylon furniture glides to the underside of the feet if desired.

22. Install a $5/16$-18 T-nut into the outside of one of the side posts, in the hole drilled in step 8. Raise the center post to a point where its slot lines up with the holes in both side posts, then insert a $5/16 \times 4\frac{1}{2}$-inch hex-head bolt through all three posts and into the T-nut. If you wish, braze or weld a handle onto the head of the bolt, as shown in the Exploded-View Diagram.

23. Mark the center post and side posts to help you quickly locate the heights you most commonly use.

Shopping List

Lumber

1 pc. 2" x 2" x 8'	1 pc. 2" x 3" x 5'

Plywood

1 pc. 5/8" x 1' x 1' A-C Grade	1 pc. 1/4" x 2' x 2'

Hardware

1	Rolling Pin 2" x 9¹³/₁₆" (roller size)	2	Flat Washers 1/4" i.d.
		2	Push Caps 1/4"
1/4	lb. Finishing Nails 8d	4	Cork or Nylon Furniture Glides 1" dia.
1/4	lb. Underlayment Nails 1"		
1	Hex-Head Bolt 5/16" x 4½"	1	pt. Carpenter's Wood Glue
1	T-Nut 5/16"–18		

Lumber Cutting List

Size	Piece	Quantity
2 x 3		
1½″ x 2½″ x 24″	Roller Stand Feet	2
2 x 2		
1½″ x 1½″ x 28″	Side Posts	2
1½″ x 1½″ x 25½″	Center Post	1
1½″ x 1½″ x 10″	Yoke	1
⅝-inch A-C Plywood		
⅝″ x 1½″ x 3½″	Roller Shaft Supports	2
¼-inch Plywood		
¼″ x 6⅜″ x 11¼″	Yoke Gussets	2
¼″ x 4⅜″ x 12″	Post Gussets	2

Project 6

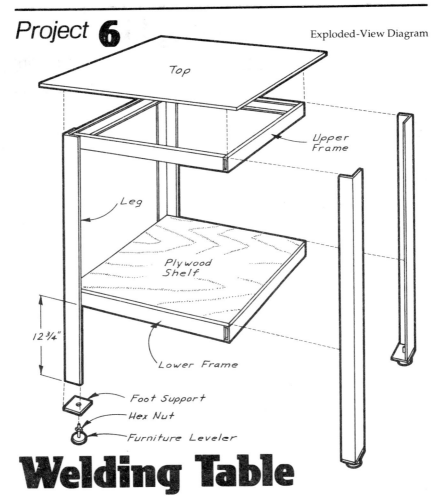

Top

Upper Frame

Leg

Plywood Shelf

12 3/4"

Lower Frame

Foot Support

Hex Nut

Furniture Leveler

Welding Table

This small sturdy table is designed primarily for arc welders, who need an electrically conductive surface on which to work. The 2-inch-wide lip around the table's perimeter makes it easy to clamp the ground cable handily, and out of the way. Other craftspeople involved in any kind of torch work will find this table convenient as well. In addition to being conductive, the top is heavy enough to act as an efficient heat sink for welding, soldering, or brazing small projects, and not likely to distort even when used as a base for larger projects requiring somewhat higher or more protracted heating. Lay fire brick on the table top for big jobs. The table legs can be individually adjusted to make the table absolutely level for accurate layout and setup work. There is a shelf beneath the table to hold small items, and the table itself is not so heavy that it can't be moved from place to place fairly easily by one person.

This is a good project for a beginning arc welder. The stock is too thick for easy gas welding. Basically, the table is built upside-down beginning with the top, which can be laid on a bed of fire brick to start if no other work surface is available. When you are finished, smooth and clean the welds thoroughly, then paint the frame with rustproof enamel before attaching the plywood shelf. Do not paint the table top. It must remain uncoated to provide good electrical contact with the welding equipment.

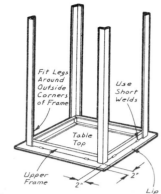

Illustration A

1. Begin by laying down the 1/4 × 24 × 24-inch steel plate which will become the table top, on a heat-resistant work surface such as a bed of fire brick.

2. Next, cut four pieces of 1/2 × 1 1/2-inch steel channel stock each to 19 1/2 inches in length, and four additional pieces to 18 1/2 inches in length, for the two frames. One frame is to be mounted beneath the table top, the other roughly midway along the legs.

3. Arrange two of the 19 1/2-inch frame pieces and two of the 18 1/2-inch pieces to form a square, 19 1/2 inches on each side, positioned on the table top to leave a 2-inch-wide lip around the perimeter, as shown in Illustration A.

4. Clamp these four frame pieces in position, then weld them to the table top. Use short welds along the sides of the frame to avoid warping the top due to heat build-up.

5. Now weld together an identical 19 1/2-inch-square frame using the remaining frame pieces. Set the finished frame aside for use in step 8.

6. Cut four lengths of 1/4 × 2 × 2-inch steel angle to 33 inches each for the table legs.

7. With the table top still upside-down, clamp the table legs in position with their ends against the top as shown in Illustration A, so they fit around the outside corners of the frame joints. Tack weld the legs in place, checking often for squareness.

8. Now clamp the other frame in place, 12 3/4 inches from the leg-ends opposite the table top, as shown in the Exploded-View Diagram. Tack weld the corners of the frame to the legs, again checking often for squareness.

9. Chip the slag from all the tack welds, then, after checking again to make sure the frames, legs, and table top are all square to each other, finish the welding by going over all the tack welds, enlarging them to full size. Continue to check for squareness between applications of the torch.

10. Cut four square pieces of steel plate, each 1/4 × 2 × 2 inches, for the foot supports.

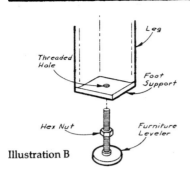

Illustration B

11. Drill a ¹³/₆₄-inch-diameter hole through the center of each support, then thread each hole using a size ¼-20 tap and standard tap wrench.

12. Weld one foot support to the end of each leg, as shown in Illustration B.

13. Install a single ¼-inch hex nut onto the shaft of each of the four size ¼-20 furniture levelers, then install the levelers in the holes in the foot supports, also shown in Illustration B.

14. Cut a square of ½-inch plywood, 19³/₈ × 19³/₈ inches, for the shelf that rests on the lower frame, as shown in the Exploded-View Diagram.

15. Finally, use a wire brush to clean all the welds of residue. Turn the table right-side-up and round the sharp corners of the top with a file to prevent injuries. Clean the entire table except the top with a degreasing/metal conditioner (available at hardware and auto-parts stores), then paint all parts of the table except the top, first with primer then with rustproof enamel.

16. Sand and paint the shelf. When it is dry, fit it into place.

17. Level the table by adjusting the heights of the furniture levelers. Lock them in place by screwing the hex nuts tight against the foot supports.

Shopping List

Lumber
1   pc. Plywood ½" x 24" x 24"

Hardware

4   pcs. Steel Channel ½" x 1 ½" x 19½"

4   pcs. Steel Channel ½" x 1 ½" x 18½"

1   pc. Steel Plate ¼" x 24" x 24"

4   pcs. Steel Plate ¼" x 2" x 2"

4   pcs. Steel Angle ¼" x 2" x 2" x 33"

4   Hex-Head Nuts ¼"

4   Furniture Levelers ¼"–20

Lumber Cutting List

Size	Piece	Quantity
½" x 19³/₈" x 19³/₈"	Shelf	1

Project 7

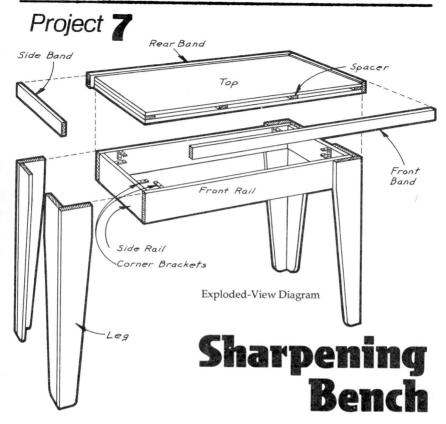

Side Band

Rear Band

Spacer

Top

Front Band

Front Rail

Side Rail

Corner Brackets

Leg

Exploded-View Diagram

Sharpening Bench

Well-sharpened edge tools are one of the keys to successful woodworking. Not many of us, however, keep the tools we use in tip-top condition because regular sharpening, especially during a project, usually means clearing a space on the workbench, setting up the sharpening equipment, and carefully watching out that the oily mess which accumulates does not find its way onto the bench top or project materials. As a result, tools become so dull that working with them is difficult and dangerous, and resharpening them, (when that occasion does finally arise), becomes a major undertaking.

In the Rodale shop, we use this sharpening bench, specially designed to be a permanent work station for all items of sharpening equipment. The bench is sturdy enough for a grinder, spacious enough for a wide variety of stones, slips, and files, and has a raised edge band around three sides which not only provides a stop to press against when using stones, but prevents objects from vibrating off the bench top when the grinder is in use. To simplify cleanup, the front side of the bench is left open.

With its heavy double-thick plywood top, this bench should function freestanding. If, however, you plan to attach a grinder which is very powerful, you may wish to anchor the bench to a wall. To do this, drill through the bench's rear rail and also through a length of scrap 2 × 4, as shown in Illustration C. Fasten the bench to the wall studs with ¼ × 4-inch lag bolts, so that the 2 × 4 is sandwiched in-between. Rubber washers, or a piece of foam rubber between the bench and the wall, will lessen the transmission of vibration.

1. Cut eight pieces of 1 × 6 (¾ × 5½-inch) stock to 31 inches each for the legs.

2. Taper each leg as shown in Illustration A. Begin at a point 5½ inches from one end of each leg and cut a diagonal that will reduce the width from 5½ at that point to 3 inches at the other end. Round the end to an approximate 1-inch radius, as also shown.

3. Assemble the legs in pairs to create four L-shaped leg units. Overlap the straight edge of one leg in each pair over the straight edge of the other, so that one outer face of each assembled unit is ¾ inch wider than the other. So that the bench design will be symmetrical, overlap the edges to the right in

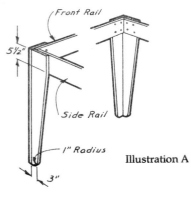

Illustration A

two of the leg units, and to the left in the other two. Fasten the legs in each pair together with carpenter's wood glue and 6d finishing nails.

4. Cut two pieces of 1 × 6 stock to 38½ inches each for the front and rear rails.

5. Cut two pieces of 1 × 6 stock to 17 inches each for the side rails.

6. Study the arrangement of the legs in the Exploded-View Diagram. Notice that the wider faces of the leg units are located on the sides of the bench. Select a pair of leg units to serve as front legs and lay them with their narrow faces down. Position the front rail on the back of the leg units so that its ends fit snugly in the corners of the legs and its top edge is flush with each unit's top edges. Fasten the rail to both leg units with glue and 1¼-inch #8 flathead wood screws. Insert four screws in a square pattern at each end of the rail, as shown in Illustration A.

7. Attach the rear rail to the other pair of leg units following the procedure used in the preceding step.

8. Connect the two sets of legs with a side rail at each end. Attach the side rails to the backs of the leg units so the ends of the side rails butt against the backs of the front and rear rails as shown in Illustration A. Use glue and four 1¼-inch #8 flathead wood screws at each end of each rail.

9. Cut two pieces of ¾-inch plywood to 20 × 40 inches each for the bench top.

10. Cut four pieces of 1 × 3 (¾ × 2½-inch) stock to 20 inches each for spacers.

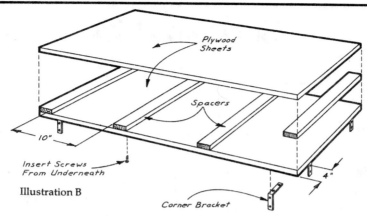

Illustration B

11. Arrange the spacers between the plywood sheets and fasten them with glue and pairs of 1¼-inch #8 flathead wood screws as shown in Illustration B. Insert all screws from the side which you designate as the underside of the bench top.

12. Attach the bench top to the leg assembly by using ⅝ × 2-inch corner brackets and 1¼-inch #8 flathead wood screws. Arrange the brackets as shown in Illustration B.

13. Cut two pieces of 1 × 4 (¾ × 3½-inch) stock to 20 inches each for side bands. Rip each band to 2⅞ inches in width.

14. Cut two pieces of 1 × 4 stock to 41½ inches each for the front and rear bands. Rip the front band to 2⅝ inches in width, and the rear band to a width of 2⅞ inches.

15. Position a side band at each end of the bench top. Set the ends of the bands flush with the front and back edges of the bench top, but allow the width of each band to extend above the surface of the top ¼ inch. Fasten the bands to the table top with glue and 6d finishing nails.

16. Position the rear band so that its ends overlap the ends of the side bands and its edge also projects ¼ inch above the top. Fasten the band to the back of the bench top with glue and 6d finishing nails.

17. Position the front band so that its ends overlap the ends of the side bands, but set its upper edge down flush with the surface of the bench top. Fasten it in place with glue and 6d finishing nails.

18. Apply a finish to the sharpening bench if desired.

19. To attach the bench to a wall, use a 2 × 4 board as packing, ¼ × 4-inch lag bolts, and rubber washers as suggested in Illustration C.

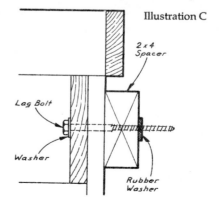

Illustration C

Shopping List

Lumber

4	pcs. 1" x 6" x 8'		1	pc. 1" x 4" x 4'
1	pc. 1" x 4" x 8'		1	pc. 1" x 3" x 8'

Plywood

1 pc. ¾" x 4' x 4' A-C Grade

Hardware

½	lb. Finishing Nails 6d		1	pt. White Vinyl Glue
100	Flathead Wood Screws 1¼" x #8		8	Corner Brackets ⅝" x 2"

Lumber Cutting List

Size	Piece	Quantity
1 x 6		
¾" x 5½" x 38½"	Front and Rear Rails	2
¾" x 5½" x 31"	Legs	8
¾" x 5½" x 17"	Side Rails	2
1 x 4		
¾" x 2⅞" x 41½"	Rear Band	1
¾" x 2⅞" x 20"	Side Bands	2
¾" x 2⅝" x 41½"	Front Band	1
1 x 3		
¾" x 2½" x 20"	Spacers	4
¾-inch A-C Plywood		
¾" x 20" x 40"	Bench Top	2

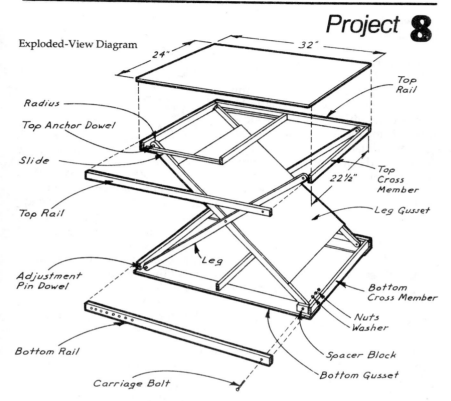

Exploded-View Diagram

Project **8**

24"
32"

Radius
Top Anchor Dowel
Slide
Top Rail
Adjustment Pin Dowel
Bottom Rail
Carriage Bolt
Leg

Top Rail
Top Cross Member
22½"
Leg Gusset
Bottom Cross Member
Nuts
Washer
Spacer Block
Bottom Gusset

Auxiliary Shop Table

This lightweight shop table is adjustable in height, which allows it to be used for a variety of purposes. Not heavy enough to serve as a main workbench, it is designed to serve as an auxiliary surface. Place it near your permanent workbench when you need extra space for hand tools and hardware. Use it as a finishing table—a place to set small objects while coating them with paint or varnish—or as an extension to a table saw, a table-mounted router, or other machines being used to cut large panels or long pieces of lumber. When remodeling

or making repairs in some part of the house, set the table up nearby and use it to hold your tools, paint, or other supplies to keep them from becoming lost in the rubble, stepped on, or spilled. If when building the table, you first determine the heights most important to you, then you can drill specific adjustment holes in the base that will allow you to quickly set the table to particular heights.

The overall design of the auxiliary shop table is simple, and its cost of construction is low. The combination of 1 × 2 lumber and ¼-inch plywood makes the table highly portable. Nylon furniture glides may be added to the bottom so that the table can easily be pushed from place to place if your hands are full. The double nuts on the ends of the carriage bolts allow the bolts to be locked in while remaining loose enough for the legs to pivot easily during adjustment. Washers provide added smoothness. Finishing is optional. Paint or polyurethane are good choices. For shop use, we left ours unfinished.

1. Cut two pieces of 1 × 2 (¾ × 1½-inch) stock to 32 inches each for the top rails.

2. Cut three pieces of 1 × 2 stock to 22½ inches each for the top cross members.

3. Assemble the framework for the top with the cross members between the top rails—one at each end and one in the middle—as shown in Illustration A. Fasten the rails to the cross members with carpenter's wood glue and 6d cement-coated box nails.

4. Cut a piece of ¼-inch plywood to 24 × 32 inches for the top.

5. Fasten the plywood top to the framework with carpenter's wood glue and 3d finishing nails. Be sure to keep the framework square.

6. Rip a piece of 1 × 2 stock into two pieces ½ × ¾ × 14⅞ inches each for the slides.

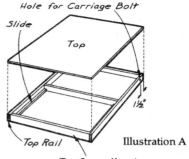

Illustration A

7. Position the slides between the middle cross member and one end cross member of the top framework, with the narrow edge of each slide butting against the inside of each rail and the bottom edges of the sides flush with the bottom edges of the rails, as shown in Illustration A. Fasten the slides to the rails with wood glue and 3d finishing nails.

8. Cut two pieces of 1 × 2 stock to 32 inches each for the bottom rails.

9. Lay out and drill a series of 9/16-inch-diameter adjustment holes on one end of each bottom rail as shown in Illustration B, unless you wish to set the table at specific heights. In that case, wait until the table is complete to determine where to drill the adjustment holes.

10. Cut three pieces of 1 × 2 stock to 22½ inches each for bottom cross members.

11. Assemble the framework for the bottom as you did the top frame-

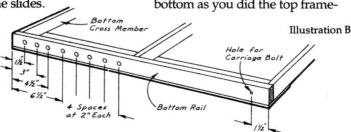

Illustration B

work in step 3. Make sure the rails are set in place with their adjustment holes parallel.

12. Cut two pieces of ¼-inch plywood to 4 × 32 inches each for bottom gussets.

13. Position the gussets as shown in Illustration C and attach one to each side of the bottom framework with wood glue and 6d cement-coated box nails.

14. Cut four pieces of 1 × 2 stock to 37¾ inches each for legs.

15. Cut a ¾-inch radius on both ends of each leg.

16. Drill a $9/32$-inch-diameter hole centered at a point 1½ inches from the end of each top rail opposite the end with a slide attached, as shown in Illustration A.

17. Drill a $9/32$-inch-diameter hole centered at a point 1½ inches from the end of each bottom rail opposite the end with the adjustment holes, as shown in Illustration B.

18. Drill a $9/32$-inch-diameter hole centered along the length of each leg.

19. Drill a $9/32$-inch-diameter hole, ¾ inch at one end of each leg, at the center of the radius. At the other end of each leg, drill a ½-inch-diameter hole, also at the center of the radius.

20. Cut a piece of ½-inch diameter hardwood dowel to 22⅜ inches in length for the top anchor. Push the ends of the dowel through the ½-inch-diameter holes in two of the legs until $11/16$ inch of the dowel extends outside each leg. Check to make sure the legs measure 21 inches apart, outside edge to

outside edge. If possible, work a little glue into the joints between the dowel and the legs. With the legs parallel, drive a 3d finishing nail into the edge of each leg to hold the dowel in position.

21. Cut a piece of ¼-inch plywood to 21 × 24 inches for a leg gusset. Position the gusset midway along the length of the legs connected by the dowel as shown in the Exploded-View Diagram. Hold the edges of the gusset flush with the outside edges of the legs to keep them parallel. Fasten the gusset to the legs in that position with wood glue and 6d cement-coated box nails.

22. Cut two pieces of ½-inch-diameter hardwood dowel to 1½ inches each for adjustment pins. Chamfer one end of each pin. Insert the pins into the ½-inch-diameter holes in the remaining two legs. Push each pin through its hole until its flat end is flush with the surface of the leg. Fasten the pins in place with wood glue and 3d finishing nails.

23. Cut two pieces of 1 × 2 stock, each 1½ inches in length, for spacer blocks. Drill a $9/32$-inch-diameter pivot hole through the center of each spacer block. Position the spacer blocks inside the corners of the bottom framework so that the $9/32$-inch-diameter holes in each are aligned, as shown in Illustration C.

24. Position the free ends of the gussetted legs on the inside of the spacer blocks, with the legs turned gusset-side-up as shown in the Exploded-View Diagram. Insert ¼ × 3-inch carriage bolts through rails, spacer blocks, and legs, then

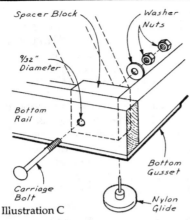

Illustration C

26. Assemble the two sections of the table as shown in the Exploded-View Diagram. Fit the top anchor of the gussetted legs into the space above the slides in the top framework. Pull the legs attached to the top framework across the outside of the first set of legs and insert the adjustment pins into one parallel set of holes in the bottom framework. Move the table top as needed to align the holes at the centers of the legs, then fasten each set of crossed legs with a ¼ × 2-inch carriage bolt, two washers and two nuts. Position one washer between each set of legs to hold them slightly apart and another washer between the inside leg and nuts.

install washers and two nuts on each bolt.

25. Attach the two remaining legs to the inside of the top framework with ¼ × 2-inch carriage bolts, washers and two nuts per bolt. Make sure the legs are turned so the adjustment pins in their unfastened ends face outward.

27. Attach nylon glides to the underside of the table bottom at its four corners if desired as shown in Illustration C.

Shopping List

Lumber
| 5 | pcs. 1″ x 2″ x 8′ |

Plywood
| 1 | pc. ¼″ x 4′ x 4′ |

Dowel
| 1 | pc. ½″ x 3′ Hardwood |

Hardware
½	lb. Cement-Coated Box Nails 6d	8	Flat Washers ¼″ i.d.
¼	lb. Finishing Nails 3d	12	Nuts ¼″ i.d.
2	Carriage Bolts ¼″ x 3″	4	Nylon Tack Glides (optional)
4	Carriage Bolts ¼″ x 2″	1	pt. Carpenter's Wood Glue

Lumber Cutting List

Size	Piece	Quantity
1 x 2		
³⁄₄″ x 1 ½″ x 37¾″	Legs	4
³⁄₄″ x 1 ½″ x 32″	Rails	4
³⁄₄″ x 1 ½″ x 22½″	Cross Members	6
³⁄₄″ x 1 ½″ x 1 ½″	Spacer Blocks	2
½″ x ³⁄₄″ x 14⅞″	Slides	2
¼-inch Plywood		
¼″ x 24″ x 32″	Top	1
¼″ x 21″ x 24″	Leg Gusset	1
¼″ x 4″ x 32″	Bottom Gussets	2
Hardwood Dowel		
½″ x 22⅜″	Top Anchor	1
½″ x 1 ½″	Adjustment Pins	2

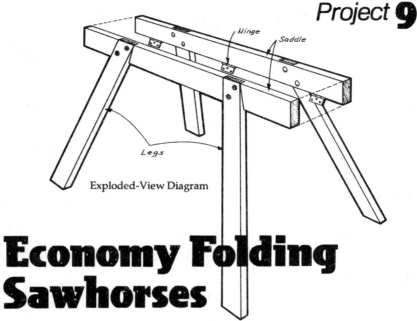

Hinge

Saddle

Legs

Exploded-View Diagram

Economy Folding Sawhorses

This sturdy pair of sawhorses was built by the Rodale Design Group to be inexpensive and easily constructed, as well as easy to move around and store. Instead of using the usual single 2 × 4 or 2 × 6 for the saddle, the design of these sawhorses features a pair of 2 × 4's turned on edge and hinged together. Thanks to this simple feature, our sawhorses can be stored flat against a wall and are easy to carry up a stairway.

The legs on our sawhorses were made from ⁵/₄ stock. With standard 2 × 4 stock, the upper ends of the legs will not be quite flush with the outside faces of the saddle as in our design.

To Build One Sawhorse:

1. Cut two pieces of 2 × 4 (1½ × 3½-inch) stock, each 42 inches in length, for the saddle, and four pieces of ⁵/₄ × 4 (1⅛ × 3½-inch)

stock to roughly 28 inches in length each for the legs. Using one leg as a pattern, scribe lines at a 72-degree angle across one face of each saddle piece where the legs will be attached, as shown in the Exploded-View Diagram. In those four locations saw and chisel out dadoes 1¼ inches deep at the upper edges and ¼ inch deep at the lower edges of the saddle pieces, as shown in Illustration A.

2. Fit the legs into the dadoes on the saddle pieces allowing the upper ends of the legs to extend a bit above the saddle for trimming later. Drill two ¼-inch-diameter pilot holes through each leg and saddle piece following a pattern that will prevent the heads of the bolts from touching when the saddle pieces come together, as shown in the Exploded-View Diagram.

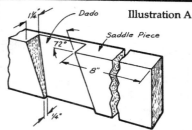

Illustration A

3. Fasten the legs to the saddle pieces using carpenter's wood glue and ¼-inch carriage bolts with washers and nuts. Use a 2-inch-long bolt in the upper hole on each leg and a 2½-inch-long bolt in the lower hole. Insert all bolts from the inside of the saddle pieces and tighten the nuts until the rounded heads of the bolts begin to pull into the wood, then cut the ends of the bolts off flush with the nuts.

4. Trim the tops of the legs flush with the upper edges of the saddle pieces. Then fasten the saddle pieces together from underneath, using a series of 2-inch fixed-pin hinges. Place one hinge in the center and one near each end of the saddle as shown in the Exploded-View Diagram.

5. Turn the sawhorse upside-down on a flat surface with the saddle closed and the legs spread apart. Measure from the flat surface 24 inches straight up to each leg to establish a common length. Draw lines across the width and the thickness of each leg to guide you in cutting the ends of the legs parallel with the top of the saddle. Trim the legs and the sawhorse is ready to use.

Shopping List

Lumber

1	pc. 2″ x 4″ x 8′		1	pc. ⁵⁄₄″ x 4′ x 10′

Hardware

4	Carriage Bolts ¼″ x 2½″		3	Fixed-Pin Hinges 2″
4	Carriage Bolts ¼″ x 2″		1	pt. Carpenter's Wood Glue

Lumber Cutting List

Size	Piece	Quantity
2 x 4		
1½″ x 3½″ x 42″.	Saddle Pieces	2
⁵⁄₄″ x 4		
1⅛″ x 3½″ x 28″	Legs	4

Project 10

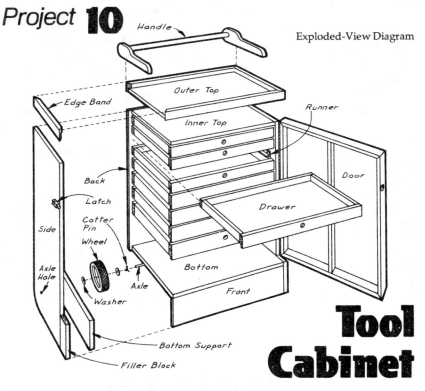

Handle

Exploded-View Diagram

Edge Band

Outer Top

Inner Top

Runner

Back

Door

Latch

Cotter
Pin

Wheel

Drawer

Side

Axle
Hole

Bottom

Front

Axle

Washer

Bottom Support

Filler Block

Tool Cabinet

This tool cabinet, modeled in part after tool chests commonly used in automotive shops, was designed by the Rodale Design Group to serve as a storage place for small tools. The cabinet has eight removable drawers, four of them 1½ inches deep, and the other four 2½ inches deep. Holes drilled into the front of each drawer provide finger pulls. The drawers may be furnished with foam or felt pads, or fitted with wooden dividers if desired, to keep tools in position while the cabinet is being moved around. Lengths of steel or aluminum angle are used for the drawer runners. We chose steel because of its lower cost. Aluminum, of course, is lighter and easier to cut.

Underneath the bottom drawer of the cabinet is an open area 6 inches high. Tools too large to fit in the drawers—such as hand planes, drills, and saber saws—can be stored here. The top of the cabinet is at a compatible height for use as a work surface, and the raised edge band on all four sides prevents items from rolling off.

The cabinet is also fitted with a pair of 6-inch-diameter wheels, positioned so that when the cabinet is upright they are not in contact with the floor. By tilting the cabinet back a few inches, it may be rolled conveniently from location to location. A lockable chest latch on the side of the cabinet keeps the door securely closed.

1. Cut two pieces of ¾-inch plywood to 15 × 35¼ inches each for the cabinet sides. Label them *left* and *right*. Label the poor-quality faces of each piece *inside*.

2. Cut two pieces of ¾-inch plywood to 6½ × 17½ inches each for the bottom supports that are attached to the inside of the cabinet sides.

3. Position one support across the inside face at the lower end of the cabinet side marked *left*, as shown in Illustration A, so the bottom and right edges of each are flush. The bottom support should extend 2½ inches beyond the left edge of the cabinet side. Fasten the bottom support to the cabinet side with carpenter's wood glue and 1-inch underlayment nails.

4. Fasten the other support across the lower inside end of the cabinet side marked *right* with carpenter's wood glue and 1-inch underlayment nails. This time make the bottom and left edges of each piece flush, so that the support extends 2½ inches past the right edge of the cabinet side.

5. Lay out and cut a 4-inch radius on the corner of each cabinet side where the support piece is flush on both edges, as shown also in Illustration A.

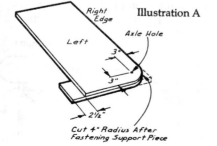

Right Edge
Illustration A
Axle Hole
Left
3"
3"
2½"
Cut 4" Radius After Fastening Support Piece

6. Locate a point 3 inches in from the side and 3 inches up from the bottom of each of the radiused corners of the cabinet sides as shown in Illustration A. Drill a ½-inch-diameter hole through each piece at that point to accept the axle.

7. Cut two pieces of 1 × 3 (¾ × 2½-inch) stock to 7¼ inches each for filler blocks. Glue these blocks on the outside front corners of the cabinet sides where the bottom supports extend beyond the sides, as shown in the Exploded-View Diagram.

8. Cut sixteen pieces of ⅛-inch-thick steel or aluminum angle to ¾ × ¾ × 14 inches each for the drawer runners.

9. Lay out and drill three ⁹⁄₆₄-inch-diameter countersunk holes in each angle to accept mounting screws as shown in Illustration B.

10. Lay out the positions of all drawer runners on the inside of the cabinet sides as shown in Illustration B. Note that all measurements are to the bottom edges of the runners. The first pair is located 2⅞ inches below the top of the cabinet sides. The next three pairs are spaced every 2⅛ inches. The final four pairs are spaced every 3⅛ inches.

11. Make the rear end of each runner flush with the rear edge of the cabinet side as shown in Illustration B. Drill pilot holes, then fasten the runners to the cabinet sides with ¾-inch #6 flathead wood screws.

12. Cut one piece of ¾-inch plywood to 17½ × 24 inches for the

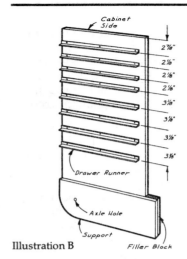

Illustration B

cabinet bottom. Fit the bottom between the cabinet sides so that it rests on top of the supports attached in step 3. Keep the front and rear edges of the bottom flush with the front and rear edges of the sides. Fasten the bottom to the bottom supports with carpenter's wood glue and 6d finishing nails.

13. Cut one piece of ¾-inch plywood to 15 × 24 inches for the inner top of the cabinet. Fasten the inner top in position between the cabinet sides so its top surface, as well as its front and rear edges, are flush with the top edges of the cabinet sides and their front and rear edges. Use carpenter's wood glue and 6d finishing nails.

14. Cut one piece of ¼-inch plywood to 25½ × 28½ inches for the cabinet back. Fit the back in position with one edge flush with the cabinet top and two edges flush with the outside edges of the cabinet sides. Fasten the back to the inner top and the cabinet sides with carpenter's wood glue and 1-inch underlayment nails.

15. Cut one piece of ¼-inch plywood to 7¼ × 25½ inches for the front piece. Fasten the front piece across the lower part of the cabinet so the top edge of the front piece is flush with the top surface of the cabinet bottom, and the ends of the front piece are flush with the outside edges of the cabinet sides (the filler blocks installed in step 7). Use carpenter's wood glue and 6d finishing nails.

16. Cut two pieces of 1 × 2 (¾ × 1½-inch) stock to 25½ inches each for the front and back edge bands that border the cabinet top.

17. Cut two pieces of 1 × 2 stock to 18 inches each for the side edge bands of the cabinet top.

18. Miter the ends of all the edge band pieces to make a rectangular framework.

19. Cut a ½-inch-deep rabbet ¾ inches wide on the bottom inside edge of each edge band, as shown in Illustration C.

20. Cut one piece of ¾-inch plywood to 17½ × 25 inches for the outer cabinet top. Fasten the edge band around the top with carpenter's wood glue and 1-inch underlayment nails. Drive the nails from the underside of the top into unrabbeted portions of the edge bands. Drive 6d finishing nails at each miter joint to hold the corners of the edge bands tightly together.

Illustration C

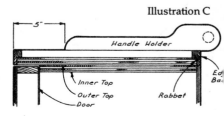

21. Fasten the top to the cabinet so that all back and side edges are flush, as shown in Illustration C. Use carpenter's wood glue and 1¼-inch #6 flathead wood screws. Insert the screws from the underside of the inner top.

22. Cut two pieces of 1 × 3 stock to 15 inches for the handle holders. Shape the edges of the handle holders as shown in Illustration D, or according to personal taste.

23. Drill a 1-inch-diameter hole ½ inch deep in the side of each handle holder to accept the handle. Locate the hole at the center of the wide end of each holder as shown in Illustration D. Be sure to drill the holes on a different side of each piece to produce a matching pair.

24. Cut one piece of 1-inch dowel to 25 inches in length for the handle. Insert the handle into the holders and attach them to the top of the side edge bands with carpenter's wood glue and 6d finishing nails. Set the front edges of the handle holders 5 inches from the front of the edge band as shown in Illustration C.

25. Cut two pieces of 1 × 3 stock to 25½ inches each for the top and bottom rails of the door.

26. Cut one piece of 1 × 3 stock to 27½ inches in length for the rail on the latch side of the door.

27. Cut one piece of 1 × 3 first to 2 5/16 inches in width then to 27½ inches in length for the rail on the hinge side of the door.

28. Miter the ends of the door rails to form a rectangular framework.

29. Cut one piece of 1 × 3 stock to

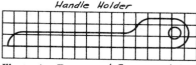

Handle Holder

Illustration D   *1 Square = 1 Inch*

26 inches in length for the middle divider of the door.

30. Cut one piece of ¼-inch plywood to 25½ × 27½ inches for the outside panel of the door.

31. Assemble the framework of the door with the divider in the middle, as shown in Illustration E. The outer edges of each rail—those that will make contact with the door panel (see step 32)—should be flush. The 3/16-inch recess caused by the narrow side rail will accommodate the door hinge (see step 33) and be the edge attached to the cabinet. Fasten the rail framework together with wood glue and 6d finishing nails.

32. Fasten the plywood panel to the outer edges of the door framework with carpenter's wood glue and 6d finishing nails. Keep the edges of the panel flush with the outside surfaces of the door framework as you insert the nails.

33. Attach a length of piano hinge to the edge of the narrow rail on the inside of the door. If the hinge is cut to a 26-inch length, it may be centered between the door's top and bottom rails. If you cut the hinge to the full 27½-inch length of the door, as shown in Illustration E, you will have to cut small notches in the top and bottom rails, in line with the edge of the narrow rail, to accommodate the thickness of the hinge before mounting it.

34. Attach the door to the right front side of the cabinet.

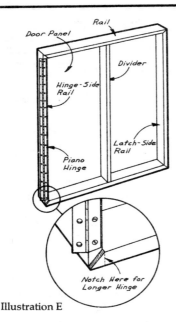

Illustration E

35. Cut eight pieces of 1 × 2 stock to 13⁷/₁₆ inches each for the sides of the shallow drawers.

36. Cut eight pieces of 1 × 3 stock to 13⁷/₁₆ inches each for the sides of the deep drawers.

37. Cut four pieces of 1 × 2 stock to 23⁵/₈ inches each for the backs of the shallow drawers.

38. Cut four pieces of 1 × 3 stock to 23⁵/₈ inches each for the backs of the deep drawers.

39. Cut four pieces of 1 × 3 stock, each to 2 inches in width first, and then to 23⁵/₈ inches in length, for the fronts of the shallow drawers.

40. Cut four pieces of 1 × 4 (³/₄ × 3¹/₂-inch) stock, each to 3 inches in width first and then to 23⁵/₈ inches in length, for the fronts of the deep drawers.

41. Cut a ¹/₂-inch-deep rabbet ¹/₂ inch wide, on the bottom inside edge of each drawer front, as shown in Illustration F.

42. Drill a 1-inch-diameter hole in the center of each drawer front for a finger pull. If desired, machine a ¹/₄-inch radius on the edges of both sides of the pull holes on all drawer fronts, using a router equipped with a ¹/₄-inch rounding-over bit.

43. Cut eight pieces of ¹/₄-inch plywood to 14¹¹/₁₆ × 23⁵/₈ inches each for the drawer bottoms.

44. Assemble the drawers so the outside edges of their sides are flush with the ends of their fronts and backs as shown in Illustration F. Make sure the top of each drawer front is flush with the top edges of the sides so that the drawer bottom will fit squarely in the rabbet. Use carpenter's wood glue and one 6d finishing nail in each joint of the drawer sides. Attach the drawer bottom to the front, back and side framework, using glue and 1-inch underlayment nails.

45. Lightly round over all sharp edges on the drawers and cabinet. Sand all wood surfaces smooth.

46. Before installing additional cabinet hardware, finish all exposed parts of the cabinet interior with clear brush-on lacquer and

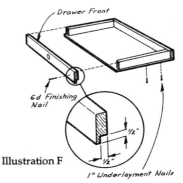

Illustration F

paint the exterior with two coats of paint or polyurethane.

47. While the finish is drying, cut one piece of ½-inch steel rod to 25½ inches in length for the axle.

48. Drill a ⅛-inch-diameter hole through the axle 3⅝ inches in from each end to accept retaining pins.

49. After the finish is dry, install the axle and wheels onto the cabinet as shown in the Exploded-View Diagram. Use a ½-inch flat washer on both sides of each wheel and hold the axle assembly in place by inserting a ⅛ × 1-inch cotter pin through each hole drilled in the axle.

50. Attach a chest latch to the left side of the cabinet to hold the door securely shut. The latch we chose has a place for inserting a padlock.

51. If desired, install ⅛-inch-thick foam or felt pads or wooden dividers in the drawer bottoms.

Shopping List

Lumber

1	pc. 1" x 4" x 8'		1	pc. 1" x 2" x 10'
5	pcs. 1" x 3" x 8'		1	pc. 1" x 2" x 8'

Plywood

1	sheet ¾" x 4' x 8' A-D Interior Grade		1	piece ¼" x 2' x 3' A-D Interior Grade
1	sheet ¼" x 4' x 8' A-D Interior Grade			

Dowel

1	pc. 1" x 3'

Hardware

¼	lb. Finishing Nails 6d		1	pc. Steel Rod ½" x 25½"
¼	lb. Underlayment Nails 1"		2	Cotter Pins ⅛" x 1"
6	Flathead Wood Screws 1¼" x #6		1	Lockable Chest Latch
48	Flathead Wood Screws ¾" x #6		2	Ball Bearing Wheels 6" dia.
4	Flat Washers ½" i.d.		1	pt. Carpenter's Wood Glue
1	Piano Hinge with Mounting Screws 1½" x 27½"		1	pt. Primer
16	pcs. Steel or Aluminum Angle ¾" x ¾" x 14"		1	pt. Latex Enamel
			1	pt. Brushing Lacquer

Lumber Cutting List

Size	Piece	Quantity
1 x 4		
¾" x 3" x 23⅝".	Drawer Fronts	4
1 x 3		
¾" x 2½" x 27½"	Door Rail	1
¾" x 2½" x 26"	Door Divider	1
¾" x 2½" x 25½"	Door Rails	2
¾" x 2½" x 23⅝"	Drawer Backs	4
¾" x 2½" x 15"	Handle Holders	2
¾" x 2½" x 13⁷⁄₁₆"	Drawer Sides	8
¾" x 2½" x 7¼"	Filler Blocks	2
¾" x 2⁵⁄₁₆" x 27½"	Door Rail	1
¾" x 2" x 23⅝"	Drawer Fronts	4
1 x 2		
¾" x 1½" x 25½"	Edge Bands	2
¾" x 1½" x 23⅝"	Drawer Backs	4
¾" x 1½" x 18"	Edge Bands	2
¾" x 1½" x 13⁷⁄₁₆"	Drawer Sides	8
¾-inch A-D Interior Plywood		
¾" x 17½" x 25"	Cabinet Top	1
¾" x 17½" x 24"	Cabinet Bottom	1
¾" x 15" x 35¼"	Cabinet Sides	2
¾" x 15" x 24"	Inner Cabinet Top	1
¾" x 6½" x 17½"	Bottom Supports	2
¼-inch A-D Interior Plywood		
¼" x 25½" x 28½"	Cabinet Back	1
¼" x 25½" x 27½"	Door Panel	1
¼" x 14¹¹⁄₁₆" x 23⅝"	Drawer Bottoms	8
¼" x 7¼" x 25½"	Front Piece	1
Dowel		
1" x 25"	Handle	1

Project 11

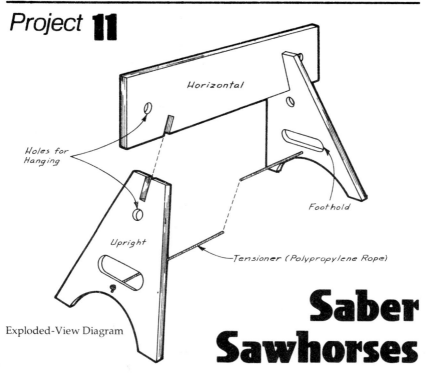

Holes for Hanging

Horizontal

Foothold

Upright

Tensioner (Polypropylene Rope)

Exploded-View Diagram

Saber Sawhorses

These sturdy and simple-to-build sawhorses are yet another product of the Rodale Design Group's seemingly endless ingenuity. Only a saber saw and drill are required to build them. No fasteners are needed: the three pieces of each sawhorse slide together for use or may be hung flat on wall hooks when in storage. A complete pair of sawhorses can be made from a mere half-sheet (4 × 4 feet) of ¾-inch plywood, any grade. Do use the polypropylene rope specified for the tensioners, however, since this type does not stretch.

To Build One Pair of Sawhorses:

1. On a sheet of ¾-inch plywood measuring 4 × 4 feet, lay out four uprights and two horizontals, as shown in the Cutting Diagram. Be sure to allow at least ⅛ inch between pieces for the saw kerf. Cut all six pieces.

2. Cut the notches, holes, and radii necessary to complete each piece, as shown in Illustration A. Be careful to make the notches exactly ¾ inch wide so the pieces will fit together snugly. To make the footholds in the uprights, drill separate large holes 6 inches apart in each

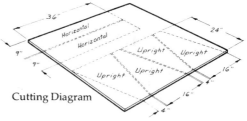

Cutting Diagram

piece, then remove the waste between each pair of holes using a saber saw.

3. Assemble the sawhorses by fitting the pieces together, as shown in the Exploded-View Diagram. Some force should be required. To steady the uprights during assembly, insert a foot in the footholds.

4. Thread a length of polypropylene rope through the holes below the footholds in each pair of uprights. Tie the rope in a knot at one end, pull it tight at the other while holding the sawhorse uprights in place, then mark the position for the second knot. Disassemble the sawhorses to tie the second knot in its proper location, then reassemble the sawhorses to make sure the rope is the correct length. Trim off the excess rope and singe the ends with a match to prevent fraying.

Illustration A

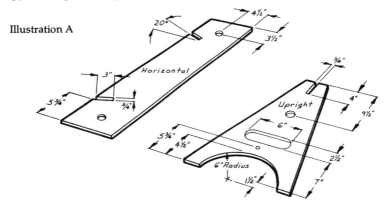

Shopping List

Plywood

1   sheet ¾" x 4' x 4' A-C or CDX

Hardware

2   pcs. Polypropylene Rope
    ¼" dia. x 4'

Lumber Cutting List

Size	Piece	Quantity
¾" x 4" x 16" x 24"	Uprights	4
¾" x 9" x 36"	Horizontals	2